Parent Like a Guru

What You Put in Your Heart
You Put in Your Child's Heart

By

Dr. Rosie Kuhn

Parent Like a Guru

Published by The Paradigm Shifts Publishing Co.

Dedication

This Book is Dedicated to Every Parent,
Grandparent, Foster Parent, and to Everyone
Who Plays a Role in a Child's Life.

You are up to BIG WORK!

Table of Contents

Introduction

Parent Like a Guru was initially created as a series of video-blogs produced in the winter of 2015. It was a shortened version of the book: ***Cultivating Spirituality in Children: 101 Ways to Make Every Child's Spirit Soar.*** I wanted to provide a version of the book that was more accessible for busy parents, guardians and grandparents, who have little time to sit and read a book, chapter by chapter. Thus, ***Parent Like a Guru*** was born.

An unforeseen outcome of Parent Like a Guru was that the blogs were rich and empowering to readers. So it made sense to create an e-book for those parents who wish to have the blogs accessible at a moment's notice. And that e-book became the book you are holding in your hands.

The intention of ***Parent Like a Guru*** is to provide stories, thoughts, and experiences that inspire and empower you to let go of everything you think parenting is about. It's letting go of how you perceive yourself as a parent, guardian, or grandparent (from here on out, collectively referred to as parents). It's intention is to support you in letting go of the stresses and the worries, plus the hoped-for outcomes of all the blood, sweat, and tears you have brought to this role as parents thus far. It empowers you to let go of doing it right, being perfect, and never failing your children, or yourself. It supports you to give up feeling like a failure as a parent. In essence, to parent like a guru requires letting go of all of that, and more.

To parent like a guru, taken on as a spiritual practice, is not about being in serenity every minute of every day or generating a "perfect" environment within which to instill everything you want for your children. It isn't even about meditating and silencing the mind. To parent like a guru does, however, require you to empower yourself to become more mindful, such as training yourself to notice your thoughts, feelings, and body sensations, as well as to notice what has you choose to do what you do.

Furthermore, another intention of *Parent Like a Guru* is to empower you to witness and become conscious of that which you really want in your relationship with your children, as well as that which you really want from your relationship with your children. Through this book, I want to empower you to be curious about you, as a human being in the role of a parent, grandparent, and guardian of all children on this planet.

By the way, I'd love for you to observe yourself without judging, without seeing mistakes, without feeling guilt and shame. Guru's are really just ordinary people who began to laugh at their humiliating and embarrassing mistakes. Over time, they just see the humor in being human. I so send this humor and humbleness your way. It's there if you need it!

Yet another intention of *Parent Like a Guru* is to remind you of that first moment when you fell in love with your child; when you were blown away by your capacity to love. Through this book, you will empower yourself to return to that love, which resides in you always, but often gets buried by the demands of daily activities, stresses, and worries.

As you read through this book, you will find yourself staying present, as best as you can, to what you believe to be your highest truth and to your highest contribution to the well-being of your children.

As parents, none of us get it right and we never get it done. What we get are thousands upon thousands of opportunities to notice when and how we do what we do. With experience and maturity, we inevitably get that within every one of these opportunities is a gift of direct experience, which reflects the degree to which we stayed in alignment with our truth, our values, our desire, and our commitment to make our children's spirit soar.

Like all spiritual practices, we cannot hurry the process, because, as most gurus will tell you, there is nowhere to go that is any better than this exquisite moment within which you are currently living. No other moment is better than this one for learning to parent like a guru.

Just for this moment, practice closing your eyes, and feel into your being. Notice the state of your being. Notice if you are being relaxed, anxious, angry, happy. These states of being directly influence how you do what you do, as a parent and as a person.

Ask yourself: "What is the state of being that I want to experience as I parent my children? As a grandparent, teacher, or guardian of children, you can ask the same questions, as all of us are being a certain way, and being influenced by our being-ness.

A second question to ask yourself: "How do I allow my circumstances to influence how I be a parent?"

Starting here, where you are, right now, not waiting until tomorrow, allows you to notice who you are now, while discerning how you want to be as you begin to parent like a guru.

Enjoy the Journey!

Chapter One
Before You Take That First Step

Stepping onto the *Parent Like a Guru* path requires that you clarify, for yourself, not only what is compelling enough to *step onto* the path, but also what is compelling enough to keep you on that path.

People are often inspired to take that first step because it sounds exciting, feels exhilarating, and worthy of the commitment. Few follow through with the second, third, or fourth step. Why? Because it gets scary when we begin to stretch beyond our comfort zone. We begin to feel the discomfort of the reorientation that is naturally occurring as part of growing and shifting our awareness and our consciousness.

What really works to keep us on the path is to know the truest desire that is within you – the one that will have you step, one day at a time, towards what you truly wish to experience, for yourself and for your children.

A client of mine, Sherry, who has many challenges communicating with her husband, shared that, what she wants for her children, is to have the capacity to clearly and openly speak their own thoughts, feelings, needs and wants. Sherry sees how she currently isn't a good role model of that ability. She feels too intimidated by her husband's judging looks to openly talk with him about what it's like to be her. And, she now sees that her commitment to raise children who share themselves easily, is what will have her practice speaking more clearly to her husband about who she is and what is really true for her.

Just for today, bring some thought to what is truly important to you, as a person and a parent. Ask yourself: What is compelling enough to have you step onto the path to parent like a guru, with full heartfelt commit-

ment and dedication? What is it that is worthy of the fulfillment of your human spirit, as a parent, grandparent, or guardian, that will keep you putting one foot in front of the other? What is worthy of the personal stretching and the potential discomfort that may follow, which will keep you walking your talk? The answers to these questions will empower you to stay inspired and committed to bring about transformation in yourself, and support and empower your child's spirit to soar.

Chapter 2
How Do I Know the Right Path to Parenting?

Quite often, when a potential client calls me to make an appointment for a coaching session, they ask: "How do I know that this is going to work? How do I know that this is the right thing to do?" The bottom line is that you don't know, and you won't know until you begin to engage personally and directly with the practice of consciously evolving yourself.

What does it require to evolve consciously?

Evolving consciously requires a degree of discipline, presence, and mindfulness to your thinking, to the thoughts you think, and to the outcome you are really wanting for yourself, and, in this case, for your children and grandchildren.

One of the intentions of this book is to keep the level of commitment pretty low. Maybe if you do nothing else, you will only spend a few hours reading this book in support of parenting like a guru. So, if this isn't the right path you won't have invested much, other than that. And, if you find that some of it resonates, and you want to actually practice some of what is suggested, then that would just be in alignment with what you want. Incrementally, you will explore and discover your unique way of approaching parenting as a spiritual practice.

One more cool thing is that, just by reading this material, you get an opportunity to notice the thoughts inside your head - the ones that let you know what you really do think and believe. You might have a different experience or perspective than what I'm sharing. So, as you attend to what is here, you can also hear what might feel scary, what might feel totally untrue for you, what might feel right on target, and what might feel fun and inspiring. As you listen to the thoughts in your head you will begin to know yourself better. You get to decide to think what you think, while you feel what you feel. If nothing else, this is a really good thing, no matter which path you take!

What's really true is that it isn't what I say that is important here. What is important is what you *hear yourself say* in response to my words and my thoughts. You have an inner guru that has a lot to share with you. My desire is that these words will stimulate a dialog within yourself, creating a wonderful relationship that evolves you and your parenting practice.

Just for today, listen for that question: *"How do I know this is the right path for me?"* and listen to all of the thoughts that may have you think about avoiding the whole subject and going back to what you feel comfortable with. See if you can stretch yourself just a tiny bit to stay curious about what is possible, even when you don't know the outcome. This is how transformation occurs. This is how we create a world where every child's spirit soar.

Chapter 3
Hope Is Not Enough to Make Things Happen

For many of us, we spend a lot of energy *hoping* that things will turn out the way we want, while we aren't actually directing our intentions, thoughts and actions into making things happen. Wishing and hoping really aren't that powerful, until we put some muscle behind them.

Think about it for a moment. What do you hope will be the best outcome for your children's lives over just the next couple of weeks? What are you *actually doing* in support of ensuring that your hope is fulfilled?

Quite often, we would rather live in hope, because, by just hoping, we aren't vulnerable to failing. If we don't make attempts, there are no risks. However without walking your talk - intentionally aligning your actions with your intentions - your hopes, well, they most likely will never materialize the way you hope they will.

To parent like a guru requires that you consider again, and again, and again, what you are willing to live for, and die for, to risk vulnerability for, and to risk failure for.

Parenting inevitably requires each of us to humbly admit that, after all, we are only human. You will face failure more often than you care to, I'm sure of it. But, by acting in alignment with your hopes and your intentions, you will incrementally cultivate awareness of your true capacity to fulfill your hopes and desires for yourself and your children. You build resilience, and inevitably you are unstoppable in the face of potential defeat.

Just for today, ask yourself this question: What and who is important enough to me, that just for today, I'll bring mindful attention to my actions and how they serve my highest values, my highest truths, and greatest desires? Just this one practice will take you along way on your path to parent like a guru.

Chapter 4

What is it That You Want for Your Children?

Many of us have a variety of wants and needs for ourselves and our children. Too often, these wants and needs conflict, and we are left feeling confused, frustrated and disappointed. We ignore and distract ourselves from this dilemma, hoping that perhaps in a few months, or years, this conflict will either go away or will be easier to deal with.

When we are clear with ourselves regarding our highest values, desires and wants, then our actions, our words and the way that we are present with our children will reflect that.

To parent like a guru, you wisely attend to what matters most to you as a parent, so that you can let go of what is perhaps lower down on your list of wants and desires. This requires that you know your highest wants and desires, so that these are attended to first.

Through the process of discernment, you begin to accept that there will be things that you won't be able to make happen. And, with that, you will focus on what you can make happen, with intention.

You might wonder how clearly knowing what you want makes a difference. A clear intention, a clear trajectory, a clear desire makes it so much easier for the destination to be realized. This is because you are using your intelligent choice-making muscles to bring about everything that's required to manifest what you want. There are so many variables that are brought into play when we just let things be as they are. With clear intentions and specific actions that align these intentions, you are far more likely to succeed. You are far more likely to enjoy the experience of fulfillment as a parent and a human being.

When coaching new clients, I often use the analogy of being a travel agent: When you want to travel to a specific destination, you contact a travel agent, or go online to Orbitz or Travelocity. The clearer you are about that destination, the more likely it is that you will get where you want to go on your terms. So it is with designing the destination for your parenting.

As you notice how you are using these intelligent choice-making muscles, you begin to choose to exercise them, stretching and strengthening them, while increasingly witnessing the fruits of your labor. You let go of what doesn't work and doesn't serve you as a parent; at the same time feeling empowered to choose with wisdom, in service to your highest desire for you and your children.

Just for today, notice all of your wants - all of them; write them down if you like. You will most likely notice that there are conflicting wants, for example, for dinner tonight, you want to fix something fast and easy, like fast food delivered to the door. On the other hand, you promised yourself that you would make more healthy meals for you and your family. This is a conflict of wants - and the dilemma arises. These everyday conflicts take energy to sort out. And, the fact is, until you are clearer with your priorities, you will constantly find yourself stressed and exhausted from managing the conflicting desires and commitments.

Again, by taking time today to list which wants are highest on your list of priorities, you will find that this clears clutter out of your head and heart. Decision-making becomes so much easier, and you will find yourself more empowered to follow through to ensure that your highest desires for yourself and your children are fulfilled.

Chapter 5

What is it That Your Children Need?

Children need to feel safe. Safety provides a sense of calm presence; with that comes the ability to relax and allow the natural expression of their being to occur. Play, creativity, fun, open connections, sharing what is really going on within them - these occur spontaneously for all of us, when we feel safe.

This book isn't meant to create more stress and pressure for you to be different, except in the ways that serve your highest desires as a parent. So what is that would need to shift for you to create safety for you children?

Consistency is a quality of presence, which brings about a sense of continuity for all of us. Consistency also brings a sense of safety, security and stability. We all need these, especially in our childhood years. With our fast pace, high stressed reality, how do we bring that consistency and continuity to our children?

A client of mine, Matt, with his 9 year-old daughter, Jessica, just moved in with his fiancé. This moved his daughter out of the school she was in, into a better school, and also into a new household with a new addition to the family-Matt's fiancé, who is expecting a child in six months. Jessica isn't herself, which is upsetting to her father. He wants her to get out and meet new children, but Jessica isn't doing well with that pressure to adjust. She is out of her element and doesn't know how to cope.

Jessica needs time to absorb all of the changes that are occurring in her life, few of which she has control over. She needs to feel the consistency of her father's love and reassuring presence. She needs her dad to encourage her without the pressure to conform to what he wants of her.

For Matt to parent like a guru, he needs to also come into himself, to find that safe place. This transition for him creates some of the same challenges that are occurring in Jessica. However, Matt, as an adult, has more life experience and life skills, which allows him to manage his reality in a way that Jessica can't, yet.

Just for today, notice how you create safety for your children, grandchildren, your students, or young friends. Consider what is consistent in how you show up with these children; notice how it is to be you, as you move through your day - how do you feel safe, and how do you create a sense of safety for yourself when no one else does?

You may notice that underlying all of the doing, you actually feel unsafe, to one degree or another - anxiousness is a strong indicator of how unsafe you may actually feel. How do you deal with these feelings? Are you assuming that your children can handle these feeling as well as you? Essentially, they can't.

Many of us mask our fears with distractions: food, substances, social media, TV, to name a few. These aren't supporting us to be with what scares us, or what makes us feel unsafe. And, quite often, our children follow our lead when it comes to numbing out, avoiding or distracting ourselves from what feels restless, irritable, and just plain bad.

To think about this today empowers you to see just what is true for you in this moment. By looking at it and discerning how you deal with your life in general and your fears, specifically, allows you to think clearly, using your intelligence-muscles to think differently, only in service to your highest values, and your highest contribution to your children's thriving.

Just for today, consider 3 ways you can bring consistency into your child's life. What three things can you implement in your parenting practices that may be just the ticket, right now - just for today.

Expanding your awareness to include these daily practice can feel like just one more thing to do. Yet, you can choose to let go of those things you are doing that don't actually provide the outcome you are wanting. You get the joy of empowering yourself to have it the way you want. Either way, it will feel like effort. And, you get to choose which effort will bring you the outcome you believe will make your child's spirit soar.

Chapter 6
Learning to Live Together

While we desire to parent as a spiritual practice, we sometimes get confused about what is spiritual - as in right-action, or right-thought, and what is not spiritual. The answers to this confusion will vary, depending on your religious training, your culture, and your family's traditions.

We are all spiritual beings here in human form, learning by engaging in the direct experience with the circumstances in front of us. Just like in elementary school, we learn best when we focus on what is in front of us. And, when our teachers are clear with the intentions of the specific exercise in front of us, we engage more enthusiastically with our learning.

Take, for example, a kindergarten teacher, who says to her students: *"Okay class: Today we are going to begin learning our ABC's. When we know our ABC's, we can begin to put the letters together to make words. And when we make words, a whole new exciting world opens up for us, full of imagination, information, and perhaps adventure. Who wants to learn their ABC's?"*

When we simplify the context of our reality, taking it down to elementary principles, we become more engaged and excited about the learning that is right in front of us.

Gurus live a very simple life, because they know that's all there is to do. They love, and they exercise their intelligence-muscles to realize and live into what is true and what is right-action, based on that truth.

To parent like a guru, living with your children, a partner and perhaps other people too, takes mindfulness to live into each moment as if there is something to learn - and, there is always something to learn, in every moment. Buddhists call this *Beginners Mind*. Today, I'd like you to consider

21

this: Love is not the same as compatibility. It's not the same as getting along and doing what is right all the time. Unconditional Love requires NOTHING from another person, or from yourself, for that matter. LOVE Just IS!

Learning to live together requires each of us to see each person's unique way of being in the world as just that - not good, not bad, not right, not wrong. There is no judging; only respecting people's personal preferences, even when they are different than yours and you don't agree with it. GULP!

Acceptance is a huge spiritual practice. Allowing is a huge spiritual practice - especially as a parent, because you have to distinguish what could be harmful or dangerous for your children, and what is the natural expression of their being, which, in essence isn't dangerous, just different than yours.

One of my favorite books for parents was written by Rudolf Dreikurs, called Children: the Challenge. It teaches parents to use their intelligence-muscles, to consider each child's own unique being in the world, and to respect their relationship with the world in front of them. It also teaches parents to allow the natural consequences of a child's direct experience with the world to be the primary teacher. This way, we parents, grandparents, and guardians respectfully acknowledge our children's unique relationship with the world, accepting and allowing them to learn from their own experiences.

Our job then becomes that of mindful and wise stewards, who make room for the expansion of our children's natural expression in the world to occur, with wise supervision present, every step of the way.

Just for today, notice your love for your children. You may have to take a deep breath and a few minutes to return to that presence of love, but it is there. Notice your style of guiding your children towards right-action, or right-relationship with themselves and the world. Notice your desire to pass on your style to them, and how you do that. (We all want to do this, so no need to feel bad or guilty about it.)

Just observe today what you need *for* your children and what you need *from* your children, and see if there are conflicts between the two. Give yourself some time to think about, to discern with intelligence, which is the priority of those needs. Just for today, practice noticing just this. There isn't anything to do but to notice.

Only through the awareness of our thinking, our feelings, our body sensations, and our actions can we consider the possibility of choice and change. So, doing nothing but noticing has the potential of creating transformation. I have no doubt about that!

Chapter 7
Who Are You Talking To?

It's All in Your Head.

More often than you can imagine, how you are being and what you are doing in this moment, or in any moment, is based solely on what is happening inside your head. You, like most of us, are not present to who is standing or sitting front of you. You, like most of us, are not communicating specifically with the person in front of you, but rather, you are communicating with your *interpretations* of the person in front of you.

In A Course in Miracles, one of the most perplexing statements shared is: **"I am never upset for the reason I think."** For decades, my response to this sentence has been, "Oh, yes I am! I know exactly the reason why I'm upset."

However, when I realized that most of the time I'm responding only to my interpretations of this person, or this situation, I was able to be more discerning - using my intelligence-muscles - to look at my situation in a way that allowed more clarity. This, in turn, allowed me to truly respond differently. Inevitably, it has led to being upset far less frequently than I could ever imagine.

All human beings have learned to create contexts (patterns of thinking and doing), which allows us to turn on our "Auto-Pilot Me", who responds thoughtlessly to each situation. These contexts are what make each culture unique. They are also what makes every family unique, and yes, they are what makes every human being unique.

We each create our own "Auto-Pilot Me" to make choices for us without us having to be conscious to every single event of our lives. This allows us to function more effortlessly. However, sometimes, "Auto-Pilot Me" doesn't allow us to consciously and mindfully respond to the unique situations in front of us. Words, actions, and emotions fly around as if they are intentional. Some are, yet, most of them are not - it's just what "Auto-Pilot Me" responds to, as an impulse, because we've empowered him or her to do that.

To parent like a guru, each of us must empower ourselves to practice noticing how we and "Auto-Pilot Me" are responding, and to what we are responding, when we are listening and speaking to our children and grandchildren.

In my transformational coach training program, I ask each new coach two questions: 1) What are you listening for when you are listening to your client?

2) Where are you listening from when you are listening to your client? These seem like weird questions, however until each coach, and in this case, each parent and grandparent are clear that we are **all** listening from a context where "Auto-Pilot Me" responds automatically, we can't actually be present to and in the presence of the individual we are speaking with. We can't choose differently until we are aware of how we are currently choosing what we choose, in relation to the thoughts we think and the actions and speaking that follow those thoughts.

Just for today, when your children are talking to you, ask yourself those two questions I mentioned above: What am I listening for? What am I listening from? Have fun as you learn to listen to yourself and to "Auto-Pilot Me".

Chapter 8

How Do I Get My Children to Do What I Want?

I suspect that you've noticed that I'm not one to give you exact "how-to's" for parenting like a guru. Because I believe you to be a wise, intelligent being, if I simply told you what to do, you would not take advantage of your own capacity for intelligent and wise presence in yourself and in your child's life.

You have a wise knowingness within - that inner-guru, which, when allowed to be consciously present in your life, sustains an ease and gentle demeanor, which is ever-present. When you are calm, you are able to reach the calmness within your child. There is no need for force. Who of us grownups operates well when forced to act against our own will? We resist being forced to act against our own will, and so do our children.

The self-revealing knowingness that imparts wisdom and guidance that you may be seeking outside of yourself is always *within* and always accessible to you. To parent like a guru requires you to look within, clearing away what interferes and what doesn't work. It requires you to cultivate absolute trust in your own self, your own wisdom. So, what needs to be different?

I Want My Child to Be Different

Our impulsive and incessant noticing of how we would like our children to be different interferes with the appreciation and gratitude for the gifts of the child in front of us.

Notice how often you would like your child to be different. List, if you will, what you would like them to do differently; speak differently, dress differently, eat differently, or socialize differently. Stay present, just as an experiment, to notice how much time and energy is spent wishing and desiring them to be different than who they are being currently.

Now, as another experiment, notice how often you appreciate your child, just as they are. Notice all the ways you are acknowledging them for the way they do what they do, say what they say, and be in the world - just as they are. Notice how you share your appreciation for their presence and their gifts.

Cultivating awareness of what is allows for appreciation and gratitude to shine forth effortlessly. When we birthed our children, we experienced them in their perfection. Over time, in service to us remaining within our own comfort zone, we desire them to be different. Most of us want other people to change so that we don't have to. Isn't that funny?

To parent like a guru, we require ourselves to cultivate awareness to see what is, as it is, without judgments of right and wrong, good and bad.

At times, I'm a bit stymied by all the various wants we have as parents and grandparents. Some of us want to be in control; some of us want to build trusting relationships that will hopefully turn into friendships along the way. Some of us want to create little us's, who emulate us, following our lead wherever and however we go. Others of us want our children to have the life we never had: be the athlete, academic, or socialite - a way of being that we could never make happen for ourselves.

Our children are their own unique expressions of Divine Nature.
They have their own style, personality, needs and wants, likes and dislikes. Much like most of us when we were youngsters, they too want to be seen for who they are. They want to be addressed with respect and care. They want to be empowered and encouraged to belong and participate in the family in their way. They want to be acknowledge for their unique offerings to the world.

When we remember that we wanted, and still want, these things too, we can then perhaps consider how to engage with our children in such a way that we - both parents and children, can receive what we want, maybe not all the time, in all ways, but enough.

Just for today, notice and acknowledge your children for something specific - something about them that makes a difference in your life, perhaps something that brings delight or brings a smile to your face. Instead of acknowledging how they are not what you want, practice expressing the absolute truth of how they are exactly who you are wanting them to be - that in your eyes they are without imperfection. This practice will serve you well in your desire to parent like a guru.

I wonder if God ever asked: "How do I get my children to do what I want!"

Chapter 9
Each and Every One of Us is Evolving

Most of us choose to go with the flow - riding the tide of evolution. What I mean is that we don't choose to actively engage directly in the process of personal evolution. Why? Because we doubt our ability to participate. How can we choose to evolve, when we don't know where it's going to lead us? Also, we don't know how to be with the unknown that is unfolding in front of us - that feels insane. So, instead, we choose to stay safe in the known, letting the Universe take care of itself. (As if we are separate from the Universe. Ha! That's funny.)

We didn't come here to live stable, safe lives, which in essence requires us to avoid self-realization and self-actualization. As much as we want this at times, no one actually gets it.

To parent like a guru requires each of us to live in this moment, fully engaged in what is. We experience directly the humanness of what is now. Delight, despair, and inevitably experiencing the delight in the despair - not to give away some of the high points of this adventure!

Life is Full of Unknown Potential

The only way we can experience the fullest potential of our lives is to live every moment as it transmutes and transforms us beyond who we thought we were. We develop self-realization and the capacity to self-actualize by courageously allowing ourselves to discover what truths we hold dear – those that are self-evident, and those that are full of bologna; then choosing to choose which ones to act upon.

Just for today, notice the many ways you are continually being nudged, cajoled, or pushed into evolution by the sheer nature of those little beings we call our children. By their presence alone, they stretch us to a breaking point. Few of us actually break; most of us just expand into greater levels of awareness, maturity, and wisdom.

Notice too, how you avoid the nudge, the cajoling and the push to evolve. Notice your resistance. Notice what thoughts, emotions and physical sensations show up as warning signs of the potential danger:

We forget that we are not separate from the evolution of Universal Consciousness. We cannot avoid change. Gurus accept change. They accept the constant shifts and adjustments. They allow themselves to experience fully the nature of being human and being the change at the same time.

As you learn to parent like a guru, you bring a courage and a stability to your children's lives, so that they become more fluid and adaptable to the changing world. You give them freedom to evolve. You give them permission to be the expression of Divine Grace, since that is what they already are.

Now, more than ever, we are able to make intelligent choices to evolve consciously. Creating awareness of how you want to choose to evolve, and how you want to teach your children to be aware of their evolution - that is the question to be with today.

Chapter 10
Parenting From Your Wounded Childhood

All of us grownups, to one degree or another, are really just children in adult bodies. Through experiences imparted to us in childhood, we carry the memories of what worked to get us what we wanted and what didn't work. We carry memories of the times we were vulnerable to abuse, to violence, to negligence, as well as to abandonment - emotional and physical.

We wish to protect our children from the hazards of childhood. We want to impart wisdom to them that we ourselves didn't get when we were their age, so they can avoid vulnerability, and the devastation that comes with it.

To parent like a guru requires that we let go of the stories and the memories that we carry of our own childhood. This is necessary so that we become present to what is, in this current situation, which may be causing the wounding of our children.

The fact is, no matter how good you parent, how much you try to protect your children from harm, they will find the trouble and challenges with which they need to tangle, in order to get to know who they are, to define themselves, and to find their own unique path on the spiritual plane and the human plane.

Yes, we want to keep our children safe from abuse and violence. However, the crux of the problem is that quite often, because we ourselves haven't healed our childhood wounds, we inadvertently pass the effects of our own wounding onto our children.

As a Marriage, Family, and Child Therapist, I saw many children who were identified as "the problem child" of the family. Almost always, that child was acting out their parents' unhealed woundings. When the parent, or parents, began to get support through therapy, the child stopped acting out. They could be themselves again. It seemed like magic - a miracle, that a shift could take place in the child so quickly. That's the way it works, though. It just does.

Just for today, notice the ways you protect your children from the dangers you yourself experienced as a child. Again, some of these may be realistic dangers. What are your fears or anxieties that you may be passing on to your children consciously or unconsciously? Also notice that perhaps there is an overwhelming sense of responsibility you experience sometimes by virtue of parenting children 24/7. It's good to notice what you are being with every day of your human life and your life as a parent. You are certainly not alone.

To parent like a guru means loving your children enough to get the support you yourself need, so that you can let go of the past, and so can your children.

Chapter 11

Surrendering the Idea of
Perfect Parenting

Quite often, I hear from parents: *"I didn't know how to parent because my parents never taught me the right way to do it."*

I know for myself that I planned on being a perfect parent. I would see what I believed to be errors on my parent's part, and planned to make sure I did the opposite. I would read the books and attend parenting classes. I would do whatever I could to give my children the best childhood possible. It turns out that it didn't happen for them, or for me, the way that I imagined. And, regardless of how it looked, I did do my absolute best to give them the best childhood possible.

There are moments when we get it right; there are moments when it feels like perfection. There may be weeks or months of blissful family moments. And, because life itself constantly evolves, and our children continue to grow, gaining awareness of themselves and the world, their thinking and their behavior will continue to change. All of this triggers unconscious responses in you, and all of a sudden you are acting exactly as your parents did. This is the moment you planned on avoiding. You begin to pull your hair out and yell: "How could this happen?!!"

Here's the Good News AND the Bad News:

We all carry patternings from our past. These patternings are embedded in our cellular memory and they create automatic responses - triggers, within us. Until we notice and take responsibility for changing these patternings, we will continue to act just like our parents, even when we don't mean to, or want to.

This is the Way I AM!

Quite often, people as parents will say, "Well, I guess this just the way I am. I'll never be a perfect parent. It's my parents' fault."

To parent like a guru requires that each of us, again, bring attention to the question: *What is it that I want for my children, for myself as a parent, and as a human being?*

We have an incredible capacity to change the things we can. We can grow the capacity to accept the things we can't, and to keep searching for that inner wisdom to know the difference.

Very few of us on this planet are truly incompetent, and incapable of change. Pretty much, the dilemma is that, with change comes growing pains. We don't like growing pains; we don't like any physical or emotional discomfort whatsoever. So, we try to change other people so we can avoid that which feels really yucky sometimes.

Over time, all the doing we do to avoid the growing pains that are inherent in being human causes fatigue, exhaustion, and dis-ease. We start to manifest aches and pains which we are baffled by, take medication for those aches and pains, and perhaps for the exhaustion too. I'm going out on a limb here to say: All of us do this, all of the time. We've trained ourselves to trade one set of issues for another.

Perfect parents be with what is, in the moment. They attend to the feelings and interpretations that arise within themselves as they be with the child in front of them. They may worry about what they are doing that could damage their children, but they know that what's most important, no matter what, is to act in their highest truth and to act in their child's highest good. That's the best we can do in any given moment.

Perfect parents confront themselves when they think they should always know what to do to parent perfectly. The truth is this: no one knows how to do the right thing for their children 100% of the time. All they can do is the best they can do in each moment.

Reading books, listening to other parents' advice, getting counseling, therapy, or coaching, can lead you to think for yourself, to discern for yourself, to know inherently within yourself that you are truly acting in alignment with your highest good and the highest good of your children. This is a very good thing.

Just for today, notice how you choose to choose to parent perfectly. What does that mean for you? What are the words and actions that you believe perfect parents say and do?

Now, again, just for today, practice letting go of trying to get it right, and just be you. Let go of thinking about what you might think you should be thinking. Just be present with your child - listening with presence (no other activities to distract you). Put down your smart phone and all other electronics. Turn them all off. Just be present to your child and see what shows up.

Because we can conceive children doesn't make us naturally good parents. To parent like a guru, we must attend to our thoughts, being mindful of how they may distract us from attending to our true desire. Each of us _can_ parent like a guru.

Chapter 12

How Can Children Be Our Teachers?

The unfolding Universe continually provides opportunities for spiritual and human evolution. Our children, just by their presence in our lives, give us many opportunities to notice who we are and how we are being; distinguishing how we choose from what we choose. We are also provided with an eternal source of courage, so we can empower ourselves to use our intelligence-muscles in ways that may differ from the culture, within which we are immersed.

When we parent like a guru, we open ourselves to returning again and again to what the Buddhists call Beginner's Mind.

Practicing *Beginner's Mind* only requires noticing your desire to control the moment with ideas, judgments, and beliefs that you know, or you think you should know, how to parent. Within this practice, we cultivate awareness of the unique qualities of being that show up in every child, and how we respond in our thinking mind to who and what is in front of us.

One of the outcomes of Beginner's Mind is that, quite often it brings a calm, grounded presence to you. It does this because you've been able to let go of all the thinking and doing, which initially created the restless, irritable discontent that may be so prevalent in your life, you don't even know it's there.

Just for today, see your child as your teacher. What wisdom do they bring to you? What, in you, needs attending to, while you attend to your children? Notice any irritability, frustration, sadness, or anger in you. Notice any other thoughts, emotions, and sensations that arise in the midst of parenting. Ask yourself the question: What thought is responsible for the emotions and sensations that are arising? By asking this question, and by discerning the answer to this question, you empower yourself to be present to yourself and your child in a way that supports evolution in both of you. This is a good thing!

Beginner's Mind allows you to be in this moment, noticing what is occurring within you that is just a thought or an emotion.

What I like about this practice is that it's an active meditation, in that, when you are attending to your child with mindfulness and a beginner's mind, you are fully present to your child. At the same time, you are aware of the thoughts, emotions, and body sensations that arise within you. This is very much like when you are driving a car: you are attending to many things all at the same time. So it is with this exercise.

To parent like a guru, we let go of the need to control the world.
By doing so, we open ourselves up to all of the exquisite moments and opportunities to expand who we are in the presence of our children. They are our little gurus.

Chapter 13

What Do You Do When
Your Child Becomes a Problem?

Generally speaking, problems arise due to influences from both inside of us and from outside of us. So what do you do when your children become a problem?

Though I've written about this in a previous chapter, I want to address it here, specifically in regard to where we focus our attention when we have "problem children."

First of all, it's not uncommon for parents who have problem children to worry about what other people will think. Our egoic-selves wants to look good in the eyes of others. We may attempt to deny, hide, or justify our problem child to others, for the sake of saving face in the community.

However, by worrying about what others think, we are not present to our child and their challenges. We are attempting to salvage our own egos, as opposed to attending to the present circumstances our children are dealing with, and presenting us with. By attending to the thoughts of others, we dismiss and minimize our own internal struggles and concerns, and those of our children.

Problem children, whose parents worry about what others think, feel unimportant and insignificant in their parent's lives. This, in itself, quite often exacerbates the problem.

To parent like a guru, each of us must notice where we are putting our attention, and for what specific intended outcome. In doing so, we become conscious of our desire to truly support our child in their time of need. We look within and outside ourselves for the resources to support us in attending to the influences that bring about the problems being faced by our children and ourselves.

Just for today, notice the degree to which you think or worry about what other people say about you, or your style of parenting. Notice when these thoughts take you away from attending to your children in a way that serves your highest truth and their highest good.

Today's practice encourages letting go of less important matters. It may require surrendering egoic needs for the sake of more important needs that live higher up on your list of values, principles, and desires as a parent. This can be scary to think about. Inevitably, it will serve your desire to love in ways that will stretch you beyond your imagination. This is a good thing.

This may be an opportunity to consider getting support from a counsellor, therapist or coach. Even the wisest of the wise individuals don't know everything about everything. Though I'm a trained therapist, with a PhD, I've reached out many times to experts who have an objective perspective. They've empowered me to see how I was contributing to my parenting challenges and to many of the challenges my children have had to face. They supported me while I worked through limiting beliefs and those childhood woundings that have kept me from parenting in a way that allowed me to bring my highest truth and my highest good to my children. I couldn't have done it without them, and you don't have to do it alone, either.

Chapter 14
Addictions to Avoid Vulnerability

Human experiences quite often have us feel good, or feel something *other than* good.

Let's face it: We don't like feeling anything but good, so we create strategies to avoid, distract, deny, and numb ourselves out when we feel something other than good. We use **substances** - food, alcohol, medications; **activities** - sex, gambling, shopping; emotional states of being - anxiety, anger, sadness; and **patterns of thinking** - rehearsing, replaying, worrying, and complaining.

These addictive patterns help us manage our restless, irritable discontent, thus relieving feelings of vulnerability -- we don't like feeling vulnerable! However addictive strategies don't assist in healing the original wounding, which causes the restless, irritable discontent.

To parent like a guru requires us to consider the degree to which we allow ourselves to live in our authentic humanness, and the degree to which we use strategies to avoid experiencing our humanness – vulnerability, powerlessness, hopelessness, and facing living in the not-knowing.

The truth is, we are spiritual beings who are here on Earth to experience humanness - all of it - not just the good, fun stuff. Each of us is here to realize who we are within this human form. We are here to remove any limitation to being the most authentic expression of our essential nature, and to live into our fullest potentiality, while in our human bodies. As we teach ourselves how to self-realize, we are teaching our children how to self-realize. This is a very good thing.

Every time we attempt to distract or numb our feelings, thoughts and body sensations, we are choosing to diminish and suppress a human expression that is longing for expression. 'Good' or 'bad' isn't a concern. Our essential nature is to be the expression of what is, in this moment, through this human form.

Just for today, notice when you feel good. Notice when you are feeling something other than good. Notice what you do when you feel something other than good. You might want to list these so you can easily take inventory of what works and what doesn't work for you to truly bring yourself to parent like a guru.

Ask yourself: *Is this strategy for managing my bad feelings something that I want to teach my children?* Then ask: *What do I want to teach to my children, so they can be with their human experiences more authentically, without the need for numbing, ignoring or denying them?*

The intention of *Parent Like a Guru* is to encourage curiosity and commitment in the you who is consciously taking on parenting as a spiritual practice. It can feel hard at times, because you are stretching yourself to include more of who you already are, yet may be afraid to realize. Growing pains create discomfort, which is natural. Patience will be helpful here. There is no hurry whatsoever.

I've learned through my own practice of parenting like a guru, that there's nowhere to go, and nothing else more important than you being with what is here now, in this present moment. We have to get through the basics of what we are attempting to learn and be with as parents. If you don't allow yourself your full presence with what you are having to be with in this moment, you will not have what you need at the next challenge either. It's like attempting trigonometry before learning how to add and subtract. It doesn't work that way!

Chapter 15
Do I Like My Children?

Remembering what it was like to be a kid growing up often allows each of us to remember what we thought and felt, being in the presence of our parents and other grownups.

Truthfully, I have very few memories of grownups actually enjoying my presence in their lives, so much so that the ones I do recall carry the experience of shock: that an adult would choose to spend time with me, not because they had to, but because they wanted to.

In the imaginings of having children of my own - and now in having a grandson, I delight in their presence. It's not just that I love them, and that I want a sense of family and of belonging; it's that I experience the wonder of being with their preciousness, with the unique way they design their reality. I like them as people. I hope they know that I like them.

To parent like a guru allows each of us to experience the quality of the being - the essence of our children as they walk into the room. This quality of being - the essential nature of each individual, is distinguished from what they do, and what they think. It's more about *how* they do what they do, and how they think what they think, which is sourced in their essence of being.

There is an exercise that I do with people: I have them walk up to, or call 10 people - some they know, some they don't know. They are to ask each of these individuals this: *"What shows up when I do: What qualities enter the room when I do?"*

Remarkably, the responses from strangers, family, friends, or coworkers are often very similar, if not the same. People see beyond our physical and emotional selves, and can put words to the *you* they experience within your human form.

One of the many values of this exercise is that barriers of judgments, perceptions, and interpretations vanish in a flash. What is left is an experience of presence, connection, and engagement with whomever is in front of you.

Just for today, practice noticing what shows up when your child walks into the room - what qualities enter the room when they do? Also notice what shows up in you when they enter the room - what qualities do you experience in yourself when they enter the room?

This practice allows each of us to witness the way we see others in our lives - especially our children or grandchildren. It allows us to watch as we create interpretations about them that have nothing to do with their essence of being, yet greatly influences our relationship with them.

It's Easy to Love the Lovable…

To parent like a guru doesn't require that we always *like* our children, because sometimes we won't. It does require that we cultivate awareness of what it is inside ourselves that create that dislike, so that we can choose consciously to be-with our dislike as ours, without making our child or grandchild wrong or bad, just because we experience dislike when in their presence. My experience is that, when I own my perceptions, interpretation, and judgments, my relationship with the other person swiftly shifts to something precious. It's the owning of my perceptions, interpretations, and judgments that may take some time to be-with, to discern, and to shift. With compassion and patience, all things unfold in beauty and delight.

And, just as an experiment, see what happens in you when you say to your child, or grandchild: *I Like You!*

Chapter 16
Forgiving the Unforgivable

I have to break it to you. You will fail to be perfect parents. Even if you act as a perfect parent, doing what is in the best interest of your children or grandchildren, there are no guarantees that the outcome will prove to be what you anticipated. Under the most loving intention, your children may not perceive your parental choices and decision the same way as you. They may see you as despicable and unforgivable. Keep breathing.

There are so many parents who have children who will not forgive them. These parents cannot find ways to heal the separations. They feel power-less and sometimes hopeless. They beat themselves up for not knowing how to parent in a way that brings about connection and love with their children. They live in hope that one day there will be forgiveness and understanding.

All we can do is the very best we know how to do, given our upbring-ing, our culturalization, and how we continue to interpret our situa-tions. This doesn't guarantee that success will prevail. However, that the choice was made with the utmost care for your children in mind, that is what matters most.

Near the end of his life on Earth, Jesus said: "Father forgive them, for they know not what they do." The most despicable and unforgivable act, in Jesus's mind and heart was still forgivable, because he saw that their level of consciousness couldn't create a different scenario than the one he expe-rienced. He expressed compassion for the way that it was, for all of those who partook in his crucifixion.

How many of us, as children, experienced wounding due to the ac-tions of our parents, grandparents, or other grownups? How many of us have completely forgiven our parents or grandparents? Some of us, perhaps. But forgiving others - seeing that they knew not what they were doing, or had the consciousness to do it different, seems like a pretty lofty state of being. This challenges our attachments to right, wrong, good, and bad.

What do we do with our judgments? How do we be with the feelings and emotions that lay underneath our blaming, shaming, and our righteousness? The unexpressed and unresolved powerlessness and helplessness that we really don't want to ever touch again, is still there waiting to be acknowledged, witnessed, and expressed?

To parent like a guru requires the cultivation of one's capacity to forgive even the unforgivable. It may require forgiving those who cannot yet forgive you, even when you were doing the very best you knew how to do. It may also require you to forgive yourself, surrendering any shred of defensiveness, righteousness, or goodness in your intentions. Sometimes forgiving yourself is the only thing left to do.

I've been one of those children who could not forgive my parents for being less than perfect - not until I was well into my 50's. I've also been one of those parents who have children that have found it very difficult to forgive me for the choices I made.

My experience as this 'unforgiven' parent brought about compassion for my mother for the way that I had continually expressed my contempt of her, in ways I thought was less than obvious. I realized the degree to which my contempt created an environment within which neither of us felt safe to be true to ourselves and to each other. Over time, I've forgiven myself and I've forgiven my mom; neither of us knew what we were doing.

I can also forgive my children for being unforgiving. Heck, like I said, I remained unforgiving of my mom and dad until both of them had been in the ground for almost a decade. **I understand that my children, like me, will need the time they need to come to forgiveness of me.** As much as I'd like it to be different, I accept their need to choose how they choose, regarding forgiveness. **My job is to continue to forgive myself for not getting it right enough to have a perfect outcome for all of us.** With that comes acceptance of what is now. What else can there be?

Chapter 17
Being in Your Presence

People pay thousands of dollars and travel thousands of miles sometimes to sit at the feet of a guru. Why?

True gurus shine as the reflection of the individual who is in front of them; they sit in unconditional acceptance and love, suspending all judgments, no matter what. It isn't so much about what the guru says; it's that they be the expression of their divine nature, and rarely anything but their divine nature. And, as I said, they are the reflection of the divine nature of the person or people sitting in front of them. What could be more simple?

To parent like a guru doesn't require you to sit cross-legged in meditation for hours on end; it doesn't require you to be wise beyond the beyond. The practice of parenting like a guru only provides you with opportunities to notice what stops you from being the loving presence for your children, even when they are acting out. It only encourages you to take a look at the thoughts and emotions that trigger reactions and responses that aren't what you want to be, do, or share. To parent like a guru empowers you to be aware of what is in your parenting toolbox, to sort out those tools and strategies that actually don't work - tossing them out, so that you have room for those new tools, the ones that actually work the way you want them to.

Just for today, sit with your children for just a minute or two - or more if you'd like, and allow them to experience the presence of your essential nature - the truth of the real you. Welcome them with your eyes and your smile, with your open heart. Let them see their own beautiful and radiant reflection in your eyes. Without a word, let them experience their own divine nature while in your presence. What could be simpler? The great part of this practice is that they won't know that you are doing something different than just loving them and being with them. FUN!

Chapter 18
Children are People

First, we are spiritual beings. Then, by choosing to come into human form, we become human beings - then our gender develops. Essentially our culturalization takes over and we are trained to think, speak, and act, according to the contexts within which we are raised. Infancy, childhood, adolescence, young adulthood, and so on, is the evolutionary process by which we grow and expand in our human and our spiritual consciousness.

Even as parents and grandparents, we carry the training, the attitudes and the perspectives that we developed through our infancy all the way to this present moment. We are children and we are adults.

All of this is to say that, how you perceive the human being within the infant, the child, and the adolescent, will influence who they become in relation to you. Your judgments and interpretations of them create and support a way of relating that quite often lasts throughout your lifetime. You are cultivating a lifelong relationship with this being, from the moment of inception. In your imagination, how do you proceed to bring about the best relationship possible with your child?

To parent like a guru, we cultivate awareness of how we are viewing the being within our child's human form. We become mindful of the degree to which we either steward them with love and respect, or we steward them with something else. We either create limitations to their fullest natural expression, or we create a safe environment within which to explore, with innocence and wonder, their fullest potentiality of their Self.

Those of us who are choosing to parent like a guru, are asking a lot of ourselves. We face many dilemmas consciously, and willingly challenge ourselves to take the path that requires patience, resilience, and courage. In the long run, quite often, turning off the straight and narrow road of parenting will bring a far more fulfilling relationship with yourself and with this human being, your child, whom you are nurturing through all of the stages of their lives.

Just for today, notice how you are looking at and speaking to your child. Can you see them as more than their bodies, their gender, their age, their preferences, and their attitudes? Can you see them as a wise soul, regardless of their age and appearance? How might you speak to this wise soul in this human body?

Exercising the muscles of intentionally seeing who is inside the human form looking back at you, takes practice. This ability to willingly create this level of awareness takes time, dedication, and discipline. It takes courage to explore, investigate, and experiment with how you are being conscious to your own set of lenses, through which you view your world, which includes you. Though this practice can be challenging, I encourage you to be curious and in wonder about you, as you parent like a guru.

Chapter 19
Being a Real Person

Our role as parents shift and change with every child and with every stage of childhood - including our children in their adult lives. We move from protector and primary nurturer to steward and guide - from someone who provides leadership and guidance, to hopefully, a trusted and respected elder to whom your children will turn when they need to feel heard and trusted in their own right.

To parent like a guru requires that we cultivate awareness regarding our own needs, and perhaps our attachments to parenting in a specific way, regardless of what our children require. It requires a surrendering to the ever-changing, unfolding, expansion, and development of our children, which continually draws us and calls us into our own potential for personal and spiritual expansion.

Just for today, notice, and perhaps write down your thoughts and feelings, your hopes and fears about parenting as your children grow and mature. Notice your desires to ignore or distract yourself from what shows up through this contemplation and discernment practice.

My experience, as a parent and a grandparent, is that accepting what is, is the most challenging aspect of parenting as a spiritual practice. Acceptance requires me to see how I want things to be different - more time with my children, more connection, more loving-kindness, and more friendship.

Accepting what is requires me to let go of what I cannot change - what I have no control over. What I can be with, and what I do have control over, is how I be with my own response to allowing and accepting things as they are; this includes my emotions of sadness, loss, disappointment, and sometimes frustration. This practice requires the process of surrendering my will, when my will cannot create the outcome that I desire. I sometimes just need to surrender my attachment to my role as parent, my identity as parent, and my dreams of what a parent/child relationship should look like.

With surrender comes serenity. With surrender comes allowing your children their fullest expression. With surrender comes an opening for you to truly realize yourself, who you are within the role of parent, and who you are outside the role of parent. With surrender comes joy, a greater capacity to be spontaneous, enjoying and loving the people you are with.

Empty-nesters know of which I speak. Parents who have lost their children to drugs, to disease, to just the process of growing and maturing & making their own life-choices, also know of which I speak.

As we accept and allow, we cultivate trust and faith in ourselves and in our children to thrive. And we all wish to participate in that thriving, in the most fulfilling way possible.

By being conscious of our patterns, our speech, our thoughts and actions, we can cultivate an awareness that allows both ourselves and our children to thrive in the fullest expression of our essential nature. This, in essence, is the art of living well.

Chapter 20
The Practice of Non-Attachment

To parent like a guru puts us on a journey of self-exploration, self-realization, and inevitably self-actualization. Self-exploration and self-realization doesn't really add up to much until we actively engage with our journey, mindfully participating in life, with our own sense of purpose at the forefront.

Most of us step onto the path of parenting with a specific destination in mind, however as we've heard before, it isn't about the destination, but the journey itself. (I always become frustrated when I hear this phrase. I don't like it. I want the destination I imagine, otherwise, what's the point?)

That we are spiritual beings having a human experience - with the emphasis on experience, is the point. Quite often, when we are traveling somewhere, we ignore the experience we are having while we are on our way to our destination; we think the journeying is just a necessary encumbrance of getting us to where we want to go.

The fact of the matter is that, in every moment of our lives, we have arrived at a destination. This moment, I've arrived here, in all my abilities and capacities, being the best contribution to the world that I can be, now. I can imagine where all of my moments will lead me, but the truth is, I have no clue. The inevitable outcome of my life is right here, now. The rest is in the hands of a greater power than me.

If I had my way, I would have been a parent who raised my children, attending all of their most important life events (well, most of them). I would have been at their birthdays, Halloween, and every Christmas and Thanksgiving. I would have put them to bed, making sure their homework was done, and their teeth were brushed. The way of the Universe took me on a different path, however, and my dream-life as a mom did not come to fruition.

I'm not alone in this reality of being an absentee parent. Because of divorce, death, disease, drugs, and any number of personal issues, millions and millions of parents do not get to live out their dreams of parenting, as they imagined.

To parent like a guru includes those parents that, for whatever reasons, are absentee parents. And, at some point, our children create their own lives, eventually making the most of us absentee parents.

Just for today, in service to your practice of parenting like a guru, notice what you are attached to, regarding your dreams of the *future you* **as a parent.** For just a few moments today, practice imagining what it would be like to be without your attachments. What would it be like to be present in your life in this moment, letting go of the trains of thought that lead you into the future - that destination that you look forward to experiencing? How would you be now, in this moment, with your children, if your focus was not on some future event you are attached to experiencing?

To parent like a guru allows you to realize there is nowhere to go - no real destination - You have already arrived. There is only this exquisite moment to be fully experienced now - this point on the path where you are standing, with extraordinary vistas of reality, which includes love, beauty, and wonder for and with your children.

For just a few moments, exercise the muscles of non-attachment. It's like learning to ride a bicycle, and letting go of the handlebars for the very first time. It takes practice, but there is joy and delight in the practice.

Within non-attachment is serenity. Within non-attachment there is the ability to truly enjoy what is, without regret or resentment for what isn't. With non-attachment there is less drama, and a greater capacity to appreciate our lives as they are. We also come to see our time with our children as precious, because we can't count on life actually getting us to a destination beyond now. Ta-Da!

Chapter 21
Right, Wrong, Good, Bad

It's fascinating to observe children as they continually experiment with what works to get their parents' attention. Though I believe all children come onto the Earth with their own unique essential nature, quite often we nurture our children to interpret their world, and live into that world, solely based on what works to get the attention they need or desire.

I'm sure that it is clear to you that, to parent like a guru allows each parent to be more present and intentional in the specific ways they choose to be with their children. You may have noticed that the more present you become with your child, the greater calm you experience in both of you. You may notice too, that there is less effort, and more ease in how you be together, perhaps playing or working together towards a common goal.

What limits our experience of love, joy, peace, and unity is only our thinking, which says we can't, or we won't. Our thinking - which includes our beliefs, judgments, and interpretations, limit our perceptual field - we create concrete constructs, which excludes the potentiality that is always accessible and absolutely present, but only when we allow ourselves to allow ourselves the possibility.

We can and we will **create greater capacities to allow unlimited degrees of connection and love, only by our willingness to consider that our thinking may be (is) the only thing that interferes with experiencing the abundance of love and grace, always.**

Descartes said: "I think therefore I am." As we evolve in consciousness, we can actually question Descartes' thesis and ask: "I think, therefore I am what? What am I thinking, and what do those thoughts lead me to believe that I am?"

Each of us, in our early childhood, as brilliant little scientists that we are, ongoingly assess, interpret, and experiment with thinking and acting, in service to understanding our world, and developing competencies, which will allow us to survive, perhaps even thrive. Our laboratory is our home and the people who live there. We decide what is true about the WHOLE WORLD based on what is happening within the structure of our living quarters.

Just for today, practice being a scientist within the laboratory of your home. Notice what your thesis is; notice what you expect to happen. (Generally, what we expect to happen is what we perceive to happen.) Practice suspending judgments, assessments, and expectations, just for a few moments at a time. Notice what happens when you drop some judgmental thoughts or words into a conversation. Through noticing and experimenting, the truth becomes self-evident. What is that truth? Inquiring minds want to know!

Chapter 22
Spiritual Phenomenon is Normal

Approximately 85% of the population of the Earth have had, or will have, a spiritually transformative experience to one degree or another. I dare say that means that most of you reading these word have had some experience of phenomenon that is beyond the explainable.

Children especially have a great deal of experience seeing angels, or having invisible friends with whom they interact. People of all ages experience synchronicities, out of body or near-death experiences, clairvoyance, and medium-ship - where people speak with those who have passed away, just to mention a few.

We encourage children to believe in the Tooth-Fairy, Santa Claus, and Guardian Angels. We teach them to pray, to give thanks, and pay homage to saints and other holy beings whom they cannot see.

The challenge for many parents is when their child has a premonition that seems implausible; or when they have a direct experience with a loved one that has died, or some other experience that is utterly impossible, yet from the child's experience, is an absolute truth.

One story in particular I'd like to share with you: *Eight year-old Katie was outside playing. She had a premonition that her mother's sister, Aunt Jessie, had suddenly died of a heart attack. Katie went inside and shared her experience with her mom Helen, immediately became enraged that Katie would make up such a horrendous story. Moments later, the phone rang, and news of Aunt Jessie's death by heart attack was given to Helen. Helen turned on Katie, angrily shoving her out of the house, threatening her of a beating if she ever told anyone about what Katie had experienced.*

I share this story with you because it is not uncommon for parents to become angry and punishing, disbelieving, and accusing their child of lying when they share their direct experience of metaphysical or spiritual phenomenon.

It's frightening for parents to hear experiences from children that are un-fathomable. And though it is frightening, the innocent child in front of you needs support and acceptance. They need to hear that you believe them and accept that what they are sharing is the truth.

There are many websites, books, movies, and scientific experts who can validate that these experiences are not usually made up by children, which can be evidenced by the degree of details they share that couldn't be known otherwise. Doctors, nurses, EMTs, hospice workers, and others who deal with death and dying on a daily basis know of the normalcy of near-death, or out of body experiences. They just aren't allowed to talk about it.

To parent like a guru allows us to be open to our children's reality. It empowers us to seek information and assistance in circumstances that are beyond our imagination, our abilities, and our control. It requires that we surrender our reality to include one that is greater than our human minds can conceive. We can support and embrace our children and their experiences, and we may need help to do so.

Adults who have had unexplainable experiences as children are often scarred, not by the experience itself, but by the sheer inability to be believed. When no one would listen, they retreated, became less trusting, and let go of an experience that could have otherwise been life changing, for the better.

You, yourself may be one of those people who had an experience that you never shared with anyone. Or, you may have heard about a relative who had an experience that couldn't be explained. It just isn't that uncommon!

Just for today, consider the ways you may encourage your children to believe in spirits, saints, fairies, angels, and holy people. Consider too, ways that you may be sharing conflicting beliefs about the unseen world. Consider how you were impacted yourself by conflicting messages you may have gotten from your parents, churches, synagogues, or other spiritual and religious organizations.

Parenting as a spiritual practice includes conversations with our children about the worlds beyond this one. It requires that we think about and find clarity for ourselves and our children about just what it is that we believe, and how to convey that in a neutral way - one that serves our children's desire to explore and know their own relationship with the unseen.

Chapter 23
The Cultivation of Discipline

Discipline is cultivated, stretched, and strengthened, only in service to bringing one's desires and tasks to completion.

To parent like a guru, we ongoingly remind ourselves of our highest desires for our children and ourselves. We accept the responsibility and the accountability that is required to ensure the desired outcome, as best as we can. We are compelled to come into right-relationship with parenting practices, enough that we willingly bring focused attention to those details that will inevitably bring about success.

We discipline ourselves in any number of ways, always in service to what it is we want. It's just a matter of deciding what we want, enough, that we begin to make the choice to bring about the outcome wanted.

It's just as easy for me to discipline myself to ignore my children's needs, in service to attending to my social network, my work commitments, the TV, because I need to, as it is to ignore my social network, work, and the TV for the needs of my children, because I need to. It's a matter of remaining mindful of my highest truth and the highest values I'm wanting to share with my children.

Quite often, when I speak of discipline, people will respond with, "Yes, but discipline takes hard work!"

What makes something hard is when we haven't totally committed ourselves to that which we say we want. We want to keep some wiggle room, just in case we change our minds.

What also makes something hard is the degree to which we've been entrained to think and act, based on a lifetime of exposure to one's consensus view of reality. We develop cellular memory based on our life experiences, which automatically responds to cues from the external world. When choosing to choose in service to a new desire, quite often it's our cellular memory along with our neurotransmitters that kick in, consistently attempting to bring us into alignment with the old patterns, usually referred to as "habits."...Discipline? What discipline?!

How do I build discipline in my children & grandchildren?

To parent like a guru brings an art to disciplining children. It's not so much that we are disciplining children; it's more that we are cultivating discipline in them as a way for them to arrive at their desired destination or outcome in the future.

Children quite often discipline themselves when it comes to sports, music, or any other arena where they have a high degree of commitment to excelling. Yet, when they are home, they may not have such an attachment to participating in family chores, such as cooking, cleaning, or taking care of whatever needs to get done, to have an effective household. How can any parent, or grandparent instill the kind of values that will support disciplined participation in the upkeep of the home? This is the question!

Just for today, notice ways that you are disciplined and able to complete the tasks that you've set for yourself. Notice where you are less disciplined, and notice where you have no discipline at all. What is it that you want enough to be so disciplined? And, what is it that is missing where you have no discipline available? What's the difference?

Just for today, notice the ways that you encourage or demand discipline in your children, or grandchildren. Notice what works and what isn't working. Consider the values that are underlying your desire for discipline in your children; are these values that your children would "buy into" if they understood that a higher value or higher good is being served through their participation? Just something to think about.

Questioning your interpretations and actions is a wonderful practice to get to know how you have learned to live life. You can empower yourself to work with your intelligence to think about what is important to you, and what you want to do about that. The only way that change can occur is through the cultivation of awareness of what is - choosing to choose what you want to be, then engaging in practices that exercise discipline, again, only in service to getting what you say you want. Yes, discipline requires exercising our intelligence-muscles, stretching and strengthening them, only in service to what you want as your outcome. Enjoy the exploration!

Chapter 24
Opening to Our Children Choosing
Their Own Spiritual Truths

Many of us who were raised in organized religions and spiritual traditions have been entrained to believe that our religion or spiritual perspectives are the right ones, the ones we believe our children and grandchildren should embrace. But what happens when our children and grandchildren don't embrace our religion? What happens when they turn their backs on the principles and doctrines that are fundamental to our way of being in the world? Some of us will become hurt, offended, angry, and punishing. Others perhaps will be accepting and supportive of their children's willingness to explore and choose, based on their own personal experience, their own principles and values.

In circumstances such as these, there are parents or grandparents who would stop all communications with their children should they choose a different spiritual path. They judge, guilt and shame them, hoping that this will bring them back into the fold. The question that begs to be asked is, what is it that gets served by choosing tactics of shaming and blaming? And, is this in alignment with what a parent truly wants with their children and for their children?

Spirituality, in essence, is a quality of being that we bring into our lives, in relation to the Absolute Truth of the Divine Presence. When we immerse ourselves in a true spiritual relationship there is no fear, there are no judgments - no right, no wrong, no good, no bad. We know in these moments that this is the way to live one's life - without fear and judgment. However, our consensus view of reality - even in regard to religion- is filled with righteous judgment, hate of the "other", and punishment. How does one makes sense of this?

Taking on any spiritual practice empowers us to be mindful of when we are in truth and love, and when we are in fear and judgment. The quintessential spiritual practice is to discern whether our thoughts and actions are in alignment with our absolute truth - love and acceptance, or whether they are in alignment with consensus perspective on religious and spiritual dogma, which conveys that there is a right way and a wrong way of being in relation to the Divine. Generally, each of us believes that our way is THE way.

To parent like a guru, we begin to trust that there are many paths to the Divine; we begin to open to the possibility that though we choose to view and practice religion and spirituality the way we do, we can allow others - including our children, to discover their own unique path and their own unique relationship with the Divine.

Just for today, notice within yourself what you believe to be true regarding your spiritual relationship with the Divine. Notice what offends you, or what you judge as wrong or bad. Notice when you judge others for how they be and what they do. What is the source of your judgement?

And, just for today, when you find yourself judging your children for what they think - especially when it comes to spiritual matters, see if you can pause your judging thoughts for a moment, just so you can become more aware of what gets served within you, by your judging thoughts.

We can experience peace, love, and kindness every day of our lives, and we can generate peace, love, and kindness in our children just through the simple act of noticing when we are in alignment with our highest knowing and our highest truth. This noticing is incredibly empowering and truly supports us creating the relationships we truly desire as we parent like a guru.

Chapter 25
Absentee Parenting Happens to Us All

Absentee parenting happens to us all, eventually. For any of us who have had something to do with bringing a child onto the planet, the relationship is ever present. Like many other aspects of life, which may get buried under the rubble of everyday stresses, we will never cease to be connected this child or to these children.

Whether it is adoption, custody agreements, going off to school, war, or, that grownup life takes children away from us, we at some time or another will experience the grief, loss, confusion, regrets, and remorse as we wade through the transition process of shifting from an every-day parent, to one that is absent to their children.

To parent like a guru brings us to accept what we cannot change. The cycle of life requires the surrendering of our role as a parent - ever present and active in our child's life, to a parent - less present and active in our child's life.

Our children go off to war. They go off to school. They go off to build families and careers away from us. We have very strong emotions around this process; so much so, that it is hard to be with these emotions, and many of us use some substance or activity to distract ourselves from what is experienced as perhaps senseless emotionality.

Being with what is, as it is, allows us to honor our connections and bonds with children we love and desire to be with. We honor the human process of separating and individuating, of our children and of ourselves. By stifling the emotional expression of what is and what we long for, we don't allow ourselves to rest in peace and in love for ourselves and our children.

When we carry regrets, resentments, hurt and torment of having our children torn away from us (for that is how it feels sometimes, even when it was the choices we made that led to the separation), we will never experience the peace and serenity that is also ever present in everyone's life.

Life is bitter sweet. In our human condition, we are faced with opportunities to experience the exquisiteness of deep love that a parent feels for their child; at the same time feeling the exquisiteness of the despair that come with the separation - regardless of the cause.

Just for today, notice regrets and longing for connection with your children, grandchildren, and also with your own parents and grandparents. Notice how you be with the emotions that surface. How do you feel about feeling regret and longing?

To accept that our human condition will always create situations whereby we are left with uncontrollable circumstances, again, even when it was through the choices we ourselves made, we immerse ourselves in the fullest expression of our essence self - we are nurtured within the deep raw truth of our human experience. It is part of our destiny to experience it all to its fullest potential. Only through the direct experience with our humanness will we find and experience peace on Earth. Only through this direct experience will we share our peace on Earth.

We, as absentee parents, can celebrate our participation in the creation and nurturing of our children, regardless of the distance between us.
We can honor ourselves for the gifts we've brought to our children's lives.
We may never know what those gifts are, but they are gifts nevertheless.

Chapter 26

I Am Grateful for the Way That It Is

Throughout our lifetimes, we are entrained to believe that what we are, and what we have, is not enough. We are taught to look for what we need to get, in order to be enough and have enough. Our mindset is of getting what we do not have, as opposed to already having everything we need.

In the book - *A Course in Miracles*, it says: *"Lack implies that you would be better off in a state somehow different from the one you are in."* If you consider the time each of us spends living as if we would be better off in a state different from the one we are in, I think you'd be blown away, as I am, by the focus of attention we give to that which we don't have, instead of to what we do have. By focusing on what I seem to be lacking, I am in a state of sadness, anger, disappointment, despair, and fear of what will become of me because I lack _____. (Fill in the blank with any number of items.)

When I turn my attention to gratitude for the way that it is, focusing on the truth that I lack nothing in this moment, I open myself to a presence of being calm and complete. I breathe a sigh of relief, and an inner knowing speaks "I am okay."

To parent like a guru allows us to practice and to experience gratitude for the way that it is. We can notice and honor the gifts that each of our children bring to our lives. We can acknowledge that, without their presence in our lives we would have missed the opportunity to learn, to experience, and to know something that could only come through this child's presence in our lives.

Just for today, say this prayer to yourself: "Oh God. I am Grateful for the Way that It Is." Notice your responses. Notice how that part of you that is so used to seeing what you lack, wants to argue with you. Notice the justifications for seeing what is missing or is lacking in your children, in yourself, and in the life you have around you. When you can allow yourself a moment or two, where you can feel the truth: that you lack nothing and you are grateful for the way that it is, notice what then arises from within, as feelings of well-being, peace and, well, gratitude.

To parent like a guru provides the experience of true knowing that gratitude is a constancy in our spiritual lives. Through parenting as a spiritual practice we begin to experience gratitude's presence effortlessly. You will be amazed when this is True for you. It is truly part of the beauty of parenting like a guru.

Chapter 27
Endings, Completions and Celebrations

As we near the end of our journey together to parent like a guru, notice, if you will what has shifted and changed? As you've been reading and absorbing the messages of this book, is there anything different in you, or in your children?

I know for me that, in writing this book, lots of stuff got stirred up; at times I was very uncomfortable - physically, emotionally, and spiritually. Poking at tender issues is not fun, but it brings awareness to some deep woundings that still require sympathy and sweet nurturing.

In reading this far, no doubt you have found yourself a bit more courageous as you stretched yourself beyond your comfort zone, embracing more of what is you, more of what is your life, which includes your children and perhaps grandchildren. No doubt too, you took a few opportunities to bypass some of the more icky thoughts and emotions that may seem too raw, too vulnerable to be with in this moment. This is good to notice, and it's good to choose what you can be with now and what may need time to heal.

To parent like a guru takes time, patience, perseverance, and courage. It takes the cultivation of resilience, so that over time you experience greater and greater degrees of sustainability of well-being.

To parade the like a guru, you are at choice to ignore and avoid this practice of parenting like a guru and return to it at your free will. You are free to choose to choose whatever it is you want to choose. You are your own wise guru, after all.

Many, many blessings to you and to your sweet, sweet children.

Acknowledgements

This Guru Series - to Parent, Diet and Aging Like a Guru began about two years ago, when, with the help of my dear friend Marj Franke, I began to create video blogs in service to parents in need of quick access to answers about parenting (Check out www.parentlikeaguru.com). After completing that series of Vlogs, we were inspired to talk about issues raised by every dieter, and thus was born Diet Like a Guru (www.dietlikeaguru.com). Aging Like a Guru never made it to Vlog status, but was a weekly article in Orcas Issues (www.orcasissues.com).

I'm most grateful to Marj for assisting me with patience and enthusiasm, not only by being the woman behind the camera, but by asking those questions that are asked by parent, grandparents, dieters and those of us who are aging. This series of books truly wouldn't exist without you, Marj!

Fred Franke, Marj's husband and my very good friend, read and edited so many of these blogs and vlogs. He is very picky in what he is willing to read, so I always felt honored and blessed by his willingness to read each piece that went into these books. Thank you Fred!

My support team, Ruby Hernandez who edits everything I write, and Maureen K. O'Neill, who has created and designed my covers, and formatted the past eight books - I so appreciate the clarity of presence that it takes to make words and pictures into a live, beautiful expression of being. Thank you both so very much!

Bio

Dr. Rosie focused her studies in Marriage, Family and Child Therapy in the 80's. In the 90's she focused on Spiritual Guidance and received her Ph.D. in Transpersonal Psychology. In 2000, she began integrating human/family dynamics with transpersonal and spiritual dynamics, creating and facilitating the Transformational Coaching Training Program through ITP, now Sofia University.

Dr. Rosie is considered a preeminent thought-leader in the field of Transformational Coaching. Her interests and passions have taken her from boardrooms to ashrams, all over the world, in service to supporting every individual to come into the fulfillment of their human-spirit. She has cultivated the capacity to soar alongside the most elite spiritual teachers in the world.

For more information about Dr. Rosie, visit: www.theparadigmshifts.com

More Books by Dr. Rosie Kuhn

Aging Like a Guru

Diet Like a Guru

Cultivating Spirituality in Children: 101 Ways to Make Every Child's Spirit Soar

ME: 101 Indispensable Insights I Didn't Get In Therapy

IF ONLY MY MOTHER HAD TOLD ME... (OR MAYBE I JUST WASN'T LISTENING.)

YOU KNOW YOU ARE TRANSFORMING WHEN...

DILEMMAS OF BEING IN BUSINESS

THE ABCS OF SPIRITUALITY IN BUSINESS

SELF EMPOWERMENT 101

THE UNHOLY PATH OF A RELUCTANT ADVENTURER

Please visit http://www.TheParadigmShifts.com for more information. To purchase books go to Amazon.com.

www.ingramcontent.com/pod-product-compliance
Lightning Source LLC
LaVergne TN
LVHW021544080426

835509LV00019B/2824